TOM, ZACK AND EMMIE IN WINTER

* by Amy Ehrlich *
pictures by Steven Kellogg

A & C Black · London

Ehrlich, Amy
   Tom, Zack and Emmie in Winter.
   I. Title II. Kellogg, Steven
813'.54[J]   PZ7

ISBN 0-7136-2958-4

This edition published by A & C Black (Publishers) Limited
35 Bedford Row, London WC1R 4JH

Text copyright © 1987 by Amy Ehrlich
Pictures copyright © 1987 by Steven Kellogg

Originally published in the USA as 'Leo, Zack, and Emmie Together Again'
by Dial Books for Young Readers, 1987.

All rights reserved. No part of this publication may be
reproduced, stored in a retrieval system or transmitted in
any form or by any means, mechanical, electronic, photocopying,
recording or otherwise, without the prior permission of
A & C Black (Publishers) Limited.

ISBN 0 7136 2958 4
Printed in Hong Kong by South China Printing Co.

CONTENTS

A Snowy Day   5

The Christmas Party   15

Chicken Pox   27

Be My Valentine   41

A SNOWY DAY

Tom, Zack, and Emmie
were best friends.
Tom was the slowest runner.
Zack was the fastest.
But Emmie was very fast too.
One snowy day Zack raced outside.
"Yippee!" he shouted. "No school!"

He ran over to Tom's house.

Emmie was there already.

"Let's have a snowball fight,"
said Zack.

He threw a snowball at Emmie
but she ducked.

Instead it hit Tom

who was coming out of the door.

"Your turn next, Zack!" Tom shouted.

But all the snowballs

Tom threw at Zack

missed him completely.

Only Zack could hit anyone.

"This is stupid," said Tom.

He walked away

rolling a snowball along the ground.

Emmie said to Zack,

"What do you want to do now?"

"How about a sledge race?" said Zack.

"We'll get snow in our boots," said Emmie.

"We could build a fort," said Zack.

"It takes too long," said Emmie.

"We could bury each other in the snow," said Zack.

"Too wet," said Emmie.

"Let's face it, Zack," she said, "we're not having any fun."

"You're right," Zack said. "Let's go and find Tom."

Zack and Emmie followed the trail which
Tom's snowball had made in the snow.
It led around a corner
and across a field.

Finally they saw Tom.
He was pushing a snowball
bigger than himself.

Four more giant snowballs
were lined up nearby.
And there was a pile
of smaller snowballs too.
"They're for snow people," said Tom.
"I want to make lots of them."

"Can we help?" asked Emmie.

"Yes," said Tom.

"But don't throw any snowballs at me." They worked until the sun went down and lights came on in the houses.

When they had finished
they had a whole snow family.
A snow mother and father.
Snow sisters and brothers.
Even a snow baby.

The snow people were wearing
their hats and scarves and mittens.
Their jackets were wet
and their boots were full of snow.
But Tom, Zack, and Emmie
did not mind at all.

THE CHRISTMAS PARTY

Every year Class Two had a big Christmas party.

"It's going to be this Friday, class," said Miss Davis.

"We'll have a tree and a lucky dip. And if we're lucky, Santa will come."

Emmie passed Zack a note.
When he unfolded it,
the note said, "Fat chance."
"What did you mean, fat chance?"
Zack asked Emmie after school.
"There's no such thing
as Santa Claus," said Emmie.
"Everybody knows that."

"They do not!" Zack shouted.

He ran to Tom's house.
Tom was outside
stringing lights on pine trees
and listening to Christmas carols.
Tom loved Christmas.
Zack was sure Tom would tell him
that Santa Claus was real.

"Is there such a thing as Santa Claus?" Zack asked. Tom took off his cap and scratched his head.
"I'm not sure," he said at last. "Why don't you ask Emmie?"

Zack gave up and walked away.
At the Christmas party
he'd find out for himself
if Santa Claus was real.

In the meantime he bought
sweets for the lucky dip
and baked Christmas biscuits
with red and green sprinkles.
Emmie came over
the day Zack baked the biscuits.

But he didn't want her to say anything about Santa Claus, so he pretended he wasn't home.

Finally it was time for the party.
Zack's biscuits were a hit
and he won a new boomerang
in the lucky dip.
But Zack didn't care.
He was waiting for Santa Claus.
Suddenly Miss Davis turned on
the Christmas tree lights
and put music on the record player.

The classroom door opened.
There stood a man in a red suit with a long white beard.
He looked just like Santa Claus.

Everyone lined up
to sit on Santa's lap.
Emmie was first in line
and Tom was second.
Zack could not believe it!

Both of them hugged Santa
and said what they wanted
for Christmas.
But when Zack's turn came
he didn't ask for any presents.

Instead he stood on tiptoe
right next to Santa
and pulled his beard.
"You're real, aren't you?" Zack asked.
"Ouch, that hurt," said Santa Claus.
"Of course I'm real."

"I knew it all along," said Zack.

CHICKEN POX

Chicken pox was going around.

Everybody had it.

Finally Tom, Zack, Emmie,

and two other people

were the only ones left

in Miss Davis's class.

All the others were off sick.

"We're powerful," said Zack. "That chicken pox won't mess with us."

But the next day
Zack wasn't in school.
Tom and Emmie went to his house
to find out why.

Zack opened the door a crack.
He was in his pajamas
and his face was covered with spots.
"Don't come too close," said Zack.
"My mother says I'm catching."
Tom and Emmie moved back fast.
"I feel strange myself," Tom said.
"I think I might be getting it."
"That means I'm next," said Emmie.

But Emmie did not catch chicken pox.
For two days she and Linda Jones
were all alone in the class.
Even though Miss Davis let them
read and draw pictures,
it wasn't really fun.

Finally people began getting over chicken pox.

The next week even Zack and Tom were back at school.

All anyone talked about
was chicken pox.
Mike said he'd had
spots on his tongue.

Polly said she'd had them
on the bottoms of her feet.
Steve said his mother had let him
drink all the ginger ale he wanted.

Rob said his father had played Monopoly with him every day.

"Poor Emmie," said Zack at playtime. "The chicken pox was great. You really missed out."

Emmie walked away from him
and sat down on a bench.
She was so sick of hearing
about chicken pox
that her head hurt and she felt dizzy.

Hey, maybe this was it!

Maybe she had chicken pox at last!

That night Emmie's mother gave her ginger ale in bed.

But Emmie was too ill to drink it.

The night after that, her father said
they could play Monopoly.
But Emmie was too ill
to set up the Monopoly board.

She had chicken pox on her knees,
her elbows, and everywhere else.
It itched like mad
and she wasn't allowed to scratch.

One day when Emmie was feeling better,
Tom and Zack came round.
They gave her a get-well card
and sat on the end of her bed.

"You better be careful," said Emmie. "I might still be catching."

Zack said, "I wouldn't mind getting chicken pox again."

"Don't listen to him," said Tom.
"There's only one good thing
about chicken pox
and Zack knows it."
"What's that?" asked Emmie.
Tom gave her a big smile.
"You can only have it once,"
he said.

BE MY VALENTINE

Tom, Zack, and Emmie were
shopping in Woolworths.
They went up one row
and down another
until they came to a row
of valentine cards.

"Oh, goody!" said Emmie. "Valentine's Day is my favourite day."

"I think it stinks," said Zack. "Only girls like Valentine's Day."

"I'm a boy and I like it," said Tom.

"You would," said Zack.

They paid for their things.
Emmie had picked out
pink hearts, red lace paper,
and gold and silver felt-tip pens.
"Come over to my house," she said.
"We'll make our own valentine cards."
"Not me," said Zack. "I'm off."
He turned right
and Tom and Emmie turned left.

At Emmie's house
they spread everything out
on the kitchen table.
Then they drew and cut and glued
all afternoon.

"I'm making cards
for the girls in our class
but not for the boys," said Emmie.

"I'm making cards for everyone," said Tom.

His cards were messier than Emmie's but they were bigger too.

Tom was very proud of them.

On Valentine's Day

he went to school early

and sneaked into Miss Davis's class.

It was so early that it was still dark.

Tom left a valentine card on each desk.

Then he went home for breakfast.

In the playground
before school started,
everyone was telling secrets
about Valentine's Day.
Some of the girls
kept pointing at Zack
and giggling.

"What's so funny?" Zack asked.
But they just giggled more
and ran away.
"I don't understand it," said Zack.
"Those girls like you," said Emmie.
"You'll see."

Sure enough,
when they got to Miss Davis's room,
Zack's desk was piled high
with valentine cards.

Everyone else had at least one card because Tom had made a card for everyone.
But Tom didn't have any.

He tried not to feel unhappy.
It had been fun making the cards.
That's why he had done it.

After school Zack and Emmie caught up with Tom.

"I'm sorry I didn't give you a card," said Emmie.

"All the ones I got were silly," said Zack. "Yours was the best."

Tom stopped walking.

"You two are my friends, aren't you?" he asked.

"Yes!" said Zack and Emmie.

"All right," said Tom.

"Then I have one more question. Will you be my valentine?"

"Of course." Emmie said, giving him a hug

"Valentine's Day is for girls," said Zack.

"Here we go again!" said Emmie.